ABUNDANT STILL

Lucy Knight

BookLeaf Publishing

India | USA | UK

Presentation by *BookLeaf Publishing*

Web: www.bookleafpub.com

E-mail: info@bookleafpub.com

ISBN: 9789358738605

First edition 2021

PREFACE

It is June 5 of 2021 and I am mulling over the fact that I had the bright idea to write a book of poetry during the final quarter of my first year of grad school…and a pandemic.

But then, what could possibly be more human than fumbling through both of those new experiences at the same time? What could force more bodily presence than the awareness of great loss and vigilance for others, and survival of self?

And so…I wrote. And much of it had to do with bodies: hunger, desire. And love. Love of family, friends. Of my dog, a constant companion through this very strange year. Of relief of walks outside or just the thought of nature during a time when many of us were stuck inside, or in one place more than normal.

I hope these poems give you some solace in solitude. Perhaps they make you smile, and maybe even think- what moves you?

Thank you for reading, and may we carry on in these glorious bodies of ours- appreciating the nature and people around us each day.

Warmly, Lucy Knight

ACKNOWLEDGEMENTS

None of my writing would be possible first without the endless support of my Mom & Dad, and my Grandmother Lucy, who have made my education possible. Rachel, you and I speak in flowers and I hope that never stops. Gelisa, my alignment accountability and intention keeper: may we always be synced..To all my Anniston family (now and former): you made me who I am by being around. Thank you.

Joy H, my informal editor and all-hours confidante: I love you, thank you, bless you for your humor from afar this year especially. To my mentor Dr. Alan Litsey, who told me to be an educator and writer ten years ago (finally!) To the professors at Tech who held space for my writing this year and encouraged confidence in it.

And to Will, who told me last year that this schoolyear would be brutal, yet he saw it as the right path and that my writing would grow: I hope you're laughing out there, with that beautiful smile. You were so right.

For William Paul, who Will always live on in my heart and in
many others'.

You are abundant Still.

1. A BEST FRIEND IS MOVING BEFORE SHE THOUGHT WOULD BE THE TIME

Life;

She will happen

All of the sudden

if you let her.

But unless you close

your porch's storm door,

she will not pass you by.

No; she enters again

with winds too

Forceful

for

That.

We are all houses

here, on land.

so we discern

who crosses the hearth..

II.

Heart begets hearth.

Wind, blows mind.

Life?

Sometimes turbulence.

Look- how a Southern

thunderstorm claps:

shakes loose

chipped leaden

paint on the blinds.

And yet your wreath

hangs firm.

Guarding its yellow

entrance- preparing

living room sunshine,

snow flurries, lightning,

June's fireflies,

long conversations,

trading books and

what precious hours

we like to think

we can harness out

from time-

to bless its next

owner; lucky

tenant.

Life brings an era's

end. Amen.

2. BRASSY

Tonight I weep for America,

Hope that this country

would choose another station

than the background

rhythm of gunshots.

Brrrop brrrop brrrr-

Take its hand off the dial-

switch over to FM:

Only a quiet wind that stirs

dreams of anything but

brrop brrr-

Cold metal and early

Death.

3. HERB OF REMEMBRANCE

This morning was woken with fog.

Heavy rain. I loved the sound, safely

shielded by umbrella. The grasses paled their greens in relief

from late springtime heat.

I stepped in a puddle and felt dirt-

silt?- attach with gravel to my feet.

Unlike the City, it was textured yet

clean. I smiled, thinking

about 23-year-old me. Hunched;

washing off in a Brooklyn tub

post-walk. That June's grimed,

glittering sidewalks.

The filth clinging.

Forcing you to scrub.

Working from home

to forget work.

Back to Louisiana, routed by

a sudden whiff of rosemary.

My hand reached down,

plucked off leaves, palms

mixing oil & herb's perfumes.

I brought my fingers to my mask;

smiled again, this time from

inhaling such a wealthy scent.

Earthy and floral, green.

The fog copied my younger

Manhattaned feet,

sticking to humidity.

So was I urged by campus: learn.

Rosemary's flowers bloom

when and where they like.

Summer:

Sun, rain, dirt, sidewalk.

4. LUCRECE (MAY YOU SLEEP)

Some nights it feels as though

I will never heal; but I always find

rest. In knowing:

No, what has been done

will never fully seal.

But I hold, heavy,

on my tongue—

the power of a poem.

I will speak for She

Whose tongue can no

Longer feel the noble

salve of words:

the dagger's

handle suddenly able

to turn outwards.

And so I pray, sharply.

That even in ancient sleep,

you were able to see—

(Though even a monarchy's

Fall would never be restitution

enough)

Your sacred body

Was the beginning

Of a revolution.

5. FORBIDDEN FRUIT

Today was Sunday.

So I spoke a prayer of thanks

to the ripe tomato

on my sandwich plate.

Eyes open,

I thought of Eve

smiling as she bit

into the red

fruit of knowledge.

Its gleaming juices

sliding down her chin.

Summer fruit fills me

like no other season's:

berries, tomatoes,

apples, peaches.

Little tastes. Sweet

bursts of original

Sin.

7. PINK MOON

Today I read: the past

would alchemize.

I laughed,

bubbles tingling my nose.

They had already been

brewing, foam gathering

in patches on my fuchsia

lungs till heading

up the breath canals

and resulting in sound.

I imagine that joy,

in these rare instances

when she aligns with the sky,

with freedom as it hangs full—

that maybe she smells powdered

fresh. She wastes no time in

fizzing the heart clean:

baking soda with an aftertaste

of vinegar.

8. NEVERTHELESS

These poems are for you

And the ways

you still teach me:

grief is a circle,

a Venn Diagram.

Not a line.

Some days, I am laughing

at what I imagine you'd say.

Others, I am soaking in the wind:

Relief from heat, sounds

that carry eyes

to moss on dogwood trees

and the finches whistling

within. I breathe in this wind

and sigh it out, because- still-

Nature defies

the fact that you are not speaking

life into words of sagacity

over the phone with me.

Some days, this makes me cry:

sobs. Heart-wrecking

tears as big

as raindrops.

Still, as I recover,

singing on long drives

I roll down a window,

lost in wonder:

how much life you

carried. How it was so

Abundant

that in the air:

You still

live.

9.

There is a wall here.

I will it to stand.

No more caving in, investing

Stones I have sanded so

tenderly.

There is a wall here.

In its cracks grows ivy, wisteria.

Hanging blossoms won of sunshine,

pruning.

There is a wall here.

And a door; carved steel

gate and key,

shuddering with each

wrong turn.

There is a wall here;

I own the properties.

Weaving flowers,

mineral rocks into one:

I welcome spring.

There is a wall here—

"April!" a shout—

suffices fears, shakes

the vines into fragrant

wind.

I will let her in. What of

Winter's fumbling

fingers?

There is a wall here.

Let spring steal the keys,

laugh,

add growth to the climbing

lilac. Immortality.

10. How A Baker Finds A Poem

You told the little boy from down the street:

Poetry leaves that sweetness,

that sour ferment

in your mouth after his tiny, sharpened

incisors split a slice's crumbs.

You know poetry feeds you full.

The same way you rise not with the dawn

but make way for her, tumbling

covers off sheets and dressing

in the shifty quiet of the late night.

You know that uncertain stillness,

small numbered hours lit by the moon.

Stomach still growling because

you have not heard or said words to anyone.

The poetry rises with the sun of your ovens.

You know the shake of your hands running before your body

to button your coat and roll your sleeves.

You know the finery of flour between

fingers. How to cradle a loaf:

punched and shaped

and now, scored with a razor.

You know the reflection of your eyes

studying degrees of heat behind glass:

crumbs separating during the bake.

The phenomenon of space

Created by a serrated knife.

The steam that you inhale

before the slice of heaven hits your tongue.

Where does poetry come from,

if not Manna,

this?

You know that a child

understands this taste

more than any other customer.

The little boy from down the street

wiped his mouth with his sleeve-

careless delight.

He waved, thanking you and

humming a nursery rhyme.

11. BEING AN ARTIST IN AMERICA

Is like making a cake for other people—

fluffy chiffon, lemon divine;

and they thank you in words

instead of money per slice.

Still, they will be

sure to say, it tastes "so pretty,

but real substance is only found in pie."

12. DEFINITIONS

And here again

we are lost in

a past outline.

Skin pulling at skin—

there is a synonym to hunger

there, if hunger

could be reminiscent.

Which would mean:

in the heat of late spring,

I was remembering those

blurry winter days when

I stored and ate up

the etymologies

of your touch.

Our words.

13. ROSEMARY'S ANSWER

If, as you say:

when we die,

we are left with ground

and not sky—

I have been looking

in the wrong direction

towards my afterlife.

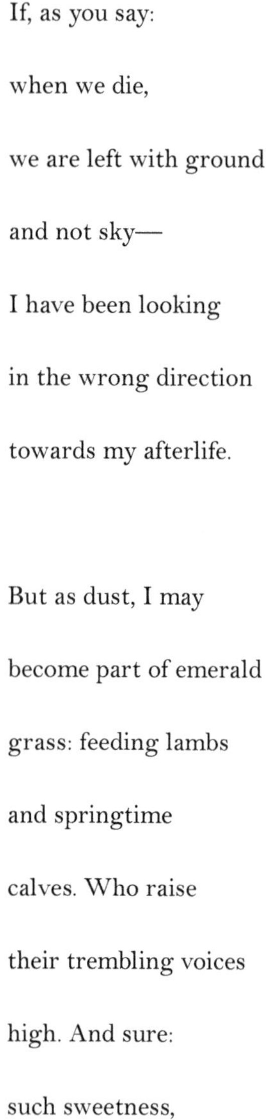

But as dust, I may

become part of emerald

grass: feeding lambs

and springtime

calves. Who raise

their trembling voices

high. And sure:

such sweetness,

meets heaven's eye.

14. OLEANDER'S HEROINE

This beauty, this little sleeping beast

lays at my side, till she noses me

to wake. Alarms a playful howl.

My mother once said

that how my hound

talks in the morning shows

her excitement at spending another

day together. I begrudgingly get out

of bed, but once dressed,

love our walks and

watching her notice, nose

each new neighborhood

flower. I don't have to guess

if gratefulness can be

taught through a wagging tail.

She prances to the door, amber eyes

aglow with sunshine.

I nose her head after returning inside.

"Good girl." She catches her treat

in the kitchen. I switch on the stove

to make mine (hot tea).

Tilting my head as I pour,

I ponder her

namesake; forced to move

through foster care. California

holds so many different homes.

When I met Astrid at the shelter

I had to leave for a few minutes

after meeting, to pay with cash.

The front desk told me when I came

back that the hound I met had tried to

follow me out. I was stunned; this shy,

sweet puppy of eight months--

adopted me.

Gratefulness? I know.

I have named her.

15. (JAZZ, EARLY AM)

Grandmother favored hummingbirds,

friendly visits in the kitchen window,

observing her lip prints on coffee cups.

Her husband loved all birds, heart of a

Scientist: notes in books of proper names,

listening to audio of calls so as to recognize

each. As I memorize lines to this little

love poem, I conjure

made up memory: both of them,

seated at the glass

table, or on the screened porch

during early hours- perhaps the children

old enough to sleep, the luxury:

newspaper reading,

leaning into a floral bench.

He is watching the seed

feeder, then smirks

and steals

a binoculared

glance at her.

She looks up and laughs.

Suddenly, a ruby throat gleams.

They turn in unison as hummingbird

Wings buzz to their tune,

low notes of desire

played through looks over breakfast.

16. FORBIDDEN FRUIT, PT. II

The man who lit the theatre

left work, middle of the day

to check on his friend.

Who happened to be a Vietnam vet;

whose backyard was a sea of red.

Nothing but a tall garden.

When the lighting designer arrived,

a cloud of smoke was all he saw amongst

crimson dots of fruit. He opened the gate

and there, sitting on the ground, was this

former soldier: high on decades past.

The designer shielded his eyes

from a glint of glass

in the sun. The soldier raised

his hand, shook salt

on a freshly plucked tomato

and took a full bite out of it.

As though he thought

it was a peach.

17. TIPTON

I have been thinking

about certain shades of blue.

About menageries

about lavender moods

about the word "Provocateur"

and what it means for a teacher

to endorse being just so.

About the ballet,

about its turn to modernity,

about sculpting each dancer's

hungered frame.

I have been hoping that thinking

about your years of impassioned

creations of light

(as life, as poetry, as play)

might inspire me to one day

be as good a teacher—

a "mother" to my students,

greeting them in moods

the color of robin's eggs,

each day anew.